These tales have been written as part of the "Chanceshire" campaign for the Cheshire-based Minister of Chance. www.ministerofchance.com

The tales are all real Cheshire myths and legends told over the years by locals and retold in books. With over 80 myths, legends, snippets of local information, plus Cheshire facts and old Cheshire words.

Copyright 2014

Contents

Introduction 8

Legends of Cheshire 9

    The Wizard of Alderley Edge 9

    The Castle and the Treasure 12

    Robin Hood's Stone 14

    The Severed Hand 16

    The Lady's Cave 17

    King Arthur and Sir Terrible 18

    The Curse of Lovell 19

    Crossroads and Corpses 20

    Gawain and the Green Knight 21

    Sir Ro the Cheshire Knight 23

    The Floating Island 26

    Lord Percy – Earl of Northumberland 27

    Hugh d' Avranches, Earl of Chester (Lupus) 28

    Bog Man of Lindow 29

    The Crosses at Sandbach 30

    The Seven Sisters Curse 31

    Ethelfleda (The Warrior Queen) and the Wedding 32

    Ethrelfleda (The Warrior Queen) and the Siege of Chester 33

History and Villains 35

    Vale Royal Abbey 35

    Delamere Park 37

    The Gunpowder Plot and Cheshire 38

    The Final Battle of the English Civil War – The Battle of Winnington Bridge 39

World War 2 Plane Crash in Hartford, Cheshire 41

The Last of the Masseys 42

Gentleman Edward (the Highwayman) Higgins of Knutsford 43

The Murder of the Princes of Wales 46

The Congleton Cannibal 47

The Deadly Duel and Church Minshull 48

Tatton Park 49

Deer at Tatton ParkCrewe Lyceum , the Railway and the Great Train Robbers 50

Crewe Lyceum , the Railway and the Great Train Robbers 51

Cheshire Minstrels 52

The Trap and the Kidnapped Mayor 53

The Old Whitegate Pub 54

Ghosts and ghostly goings on 55

Haunted Stile of Macclesfield 55

The ghost of the Roman Soldier 56

Ghostly Horsemen 57

The Weeing Ghosts of Warrington 58

Spectral Hounds and Big Cats of Cheshire 59

The lady ghosts of Marbury Hall 61

The Headless Woman of Tarvin 64

The Gately Groaner 65

The Chester Leyline 66

The Headless Duck 67

The Real and Fake Ghosts of Davenham 68

The Ghost in a Bottle 69

The Ghost of Anne Boleyn 70

River Ghost of Chester 71

Boggarts of Cheshire 72

The Unfillable Hole.. 73

Little Moreton Hall Ghostly Goings On 74

Maggoty Johnson... 75

The Ghostly Raven of Coppenhall 77

Old Laws, Cures and Customs 78

Strange old law of Chester 78

Wedding Ropes 79

Old Cures and Customs of Cheshire.. 80

May Day in Cheshire 82

Riding the Stang 83

Paternal Madness 84

Healing Well of Delamere 85

Creatures of Cheshire 86

The Singing Mermaid of Blackrock... 86

Nellie Longarms 87

The Dragon of Moston 88

The Giant of Hale 89

The Asrai 90

The Changeling of Mottram 92

The Mermaid and the Bell 94

The Blacksmith Who Killed A Griffin 95

The Doctor and the Devil 96

The Devil and the Church.. 97

Billy Hobby's Well, Chester 98

Prince Henry and the Werewolf 99
All the rest......100
    Jodrell Bank......100
    Salt in Cheshire 101
    Cheshire Cat......102
    Smuggling, Wrecking and Sea Folklore 103
    Hack Green Secret Nuclear Bunker......105
    Lady Beswick's Mummy 106
    Bridget the Witch......107
    The Statue Tried for Murder 108
    The Prophet Robert Nixon 109
    Folly Mill......111
    Anderton Boat Lift 112
    Mad Allen's Hole 113
    The History of the Stamford Lodge Site 114
    Peckforton Cyclone 116
Cheshire Facts 117
Old Cheshire Words 118
Bibliography 122

Introduction

Cheshire is a green and mainly rural county sheltered on two sides by mountain ranges. Among the tranquil green fields, there are forests and areas of woodland, castles, manor houses, old abbeys, and old market towns and villages. The fortified city of Chester is the county town.

Cheshire may appear to be a peaceful and tranquil place, but it is a place steeped in history. There are tales of battles, the onslaught of industry and lots of myths and legends along the way. Among other things, there are tales of witches, ghosts, wizards, werewolves, prophets and mermaids.

It's no surprise that this unique place continues to be an inspiration to writers and story tellers. For instance, Lewis Carroll came from the Shire and inspired him to write "Alice in Wonderland ".

Legends of Cheshire

The Wizard of Alderley Edge

There are various locations around Great Britain that lay claim to the legendary Camelot and the Knights of the Round Table. One such location is Alderley Edge, which just happens to be part of Cheshire. This village now boasts a large population of millionaires (mainly footballers and TV stars), but the edge itself still maintains its mysterious atmosphere. There are ancient mining works along the edge and a rumoured honey comb of caves that extend under the ground. It is said that a wizard roams the edge watching over sleeping knights ready for when they will awaken and save the country in a time of great danger.

Here is how the legend began.... In around the year 1696, a farmer was on his way to the nearby market town of Macclesfield when he came across a strange old man asking to buy the horse he was taking to market. The farmer refused, but was warned by the old man that he would not sell the horse at the market that day and that they would meet again that night. To the farmer's surprise, the old man's words came true.

On his way home again with the horse that night, he was again approached by the old man and was told to follow him. Nervously the farmer followed to man to a blank rock face. The old man struck the rock with his staff and the rocks parted to reveal a hidden doorway. They entered the cave with the horse and to the farmer's shock there were numerous knights and horses inside, and they were in a kind of deep sleep; one knight was noticeably missing a horse and therefore needed the one he was selling.

The old man told him to take as many gold pieces (that were lying around the cave) as he wanted for payment. The farmer then fled the cave with his payment and the doorway closed shut behind him. Since that day there have been numerous sightings of a mysterious old man (also known as Merlin) in the area, but nobody else has ever been inside the cave where King Arthur and his faithful knights lie waiting for their time to act.

Holy well, Alderley Edge- one entrance to the cave of sleeping knights

The Castle and the Treasure

Standing on two prominent hills on the Cheshire plain are the Castles of Beeston and Peckforton. On a good day you can see across eight counties, and can see the Pennines and the Welsh mountains.

Beeston castle is the older of the two castles and was built in the 1220s by the 6th Earl of Chester upon his return from the Crusades (Peckforton castle is actually a Victorian mansion that was built in imitation of a medieval castle and has been used as the set for films and television shows).

There are some conflicting stories about how the treasure got into the well at Beeston, but it is said that Royalist forces, during a battle, flung treasure belonging to King Richard II into the deep well in Beeston castle before they surrendered to the Parliamentarian army. The well is rumoured to be 370ft deep and if the treasure is there, it has still to be recovered.

There were numerous expeditions but nothing was found; however a recent blockage in the well has been discovered at 250ft, so it is possible it lies below that. Some believe there is some sort of curse on the treasure and that anyone who goes down the well will be struck dumb or go mad.

Beeston castle

Robin Hood's Stone

Back in the days of Robin Hood, the forests in the heart of England were much more extensive than they are today. Robin Hood was a frequent visitor to Cheshire.

In Tilston Fearnell, there is a barrow called "Robin Hood's Barrow", where Robin is reputed to have stood and fired an arrow towards Beeston Crag.

During one visit to Longendale (the area of Cheshire he visited most often), he met a young man who was upset about a forced separation from his betrothed; she had been shut up in a castle, by her guardian, to keep them apart. Robin sent Friar Tuck to speak to the girl's guardian, an evil baron, to try to resolve the matter. The baron said he would release the girl to marry the young man only if a series of impossible tasks could be completed by Robin. Little John would have preferred to have blasted through the castle gates and rescue the girl by force, putting an arrow through the Baron for good measure; however, Robin dismissed that idea and decided to go ahead with the tasks.

The first task was to three arrows and hit the Druid stones (now known as Robin Hood's Picking Rods). Robin missed with the first two arrows, but hit the target squarely with the third. The arrow hit with such force that it left behind a mark that can still be seen.

The next task was to dislodge a huge boulder, by lifting it unassisted, and flinging it into the valley below. Some of Robin's men tried and failed, but then Robin succeeded in dislodging the huge boulder and sent it crashing down (some say he must have had some super natural assistance to achieve that task). Not to be outdone, Little John then threw a slightly smaller boulder, which travelled a bit further, but broke into smaller pieces. The pieces lie there still and the large piece is known as Robin Hood's stone and the smaller is Little John's stone.

With the tasks completed, Robin Hood and his merry men had freed the girl so that she could finally marry her love.

The Severed Hand

Capesthorne Hall is a magnificent old house in Cheshire, owned by the Bromley-Davenport family, and is said to have several ghosts in the vault that lies in the family chapel.

In 1958, William Bromley-Davenport was awakened by his bedroom window rattling. He nervously looked out and there was a hand scratching at the glass on the outside. It was floating in mid air and was severed at the wrist.

William ran to the window and flung it open, but the hand had disappeared. He did not sleep for the rest of the night because he kept imagining the scratching of the fingernails of the hand against the window.

Theories of it being a practical joke were discounted due to the height of the window (30 foot above an open courtyard) and an absence of any window ledges.

Some time later, a well know MP stayed over at the house and had a sleepless night when his bedroom door kept opening and closing of its own accord, despite being wedged. Not sure who the MP was, but hopefully on that occasion, it was just a practical joke...

The Lady's Cave

In the middle ages, Hilbre Island was known as St Hildeburga's Ey, and there was just one monk who lived on the island.

One stormy day, the monk came out of his cave and along the shore found a young woman lying unconscious on a shelf of rock. He took her back to his cave and revived her.

When she had recovered a little, she told him that she was the daughter of the Lord of Shotwick and that she had fallen in love with a young knight, but her father would not allow the marriage. He threatened her with being sent to a nunnery and bullied her to end her relationship.

One day, her father was suspiciously nice to her and invited her out on a sailing trip, a storm brewed and her father showed her a letter saying her knight had died. She threw herself overboard and her father frantically called out to her to say that the letter was just a fake, but it was too late and she was too far away to get her back onboard the boat.

Despite the monk's efforts, the lady died in the cave and it then became known as the Lady's Cave.

King Arthur and Sir Terrible

Arthurian legend is connected to the area with the wizard of Alderley, and the popular rumour that the county Lancashire actually takes its name from Lancelot's shire.

This story is set in Longendale, where Arthur was celebrating after a great victory in Wigan. An old lady turned up at the celebrations and asked for help because her granddaughter had been kidnapped by Sir Terrible; who had already slain two potential rescuers.

A young squire stepped forward to take the challenge. The challenge was accepted by Sir Terrible who asked to face the young squire on level ground. However, on the way there, the young man was charged at from the back by Sir Terrible. Luckily for him, King Arthur had been watching nearby, and jumped out, pushed the squire safely out of the way and killed Sir Terrible.

The young lady was released and all the land and castle given to the squire, who then married the granddaughter.

The Curse of Lovell

"The cat, the rat and Lovel the dog, Rule all England under a hog"

This famous rhyme was about Catesby (the cat), Lord Ratcliffe of Ordsall Hall (the rat), Richard III (the hog; he had a boar on his crest), and Francis Lovel, or Lovell (the dog).

One day Francis Lovell, the son of the brave Sir John Lovell, was walking in his woods at Mottram when he was approached by an old hag. She cursed him saying he would never have any children and that he would have an early un-heroic death.

Lovell fought alongside the king in the battle of Bosworth and then fled to Flanders, returning as a supporter of the pretender Lambert Simnel. In the battle of Stoke in 1487, Lovell was last seen swimming his horse across a river to escape the battle. Some say he was killed in that battle, but there is an alternative story…

Lovell had no friends and trusted nobody (not even his own servants), so he crept into his house late at night and hid in a secret chamber. However the door jammed and he got trapped inside.

In the 18th century, workmen repairing the building accidentally broke into the chamber where they found a skeleton sitting at a table resting its hand on a bundle of papers. Before they could do anything, the fresh air made the skeleton and the papers crumble to dust…nobody will know what was written on those papers.

Crossroads and Corpses

Crossroads have often been thought of as mystical and spiritual places. This is partly due to the choices they represent, but also because murderers and suicides were often buried at crossroads as they were expected to rise as ghosts. Superstition said that the ghosts would not be able to haunt anyone because they would not know what path to take back to the town or village.

In Cheshire, vampires and ghosts were once thought of as being the same thing, so wooden stakes were hammered into the hearts of the corpses. In Stockport, the crossroads near to Vernon Park museum were excavated and there were skeletons underneath with stakes still present in their chests.

Criminals and witches were often executed at crossroads and gibbets hung there. Back in the days before street lights and motorcars, crossroads would have been very creepy places indeed!

Gawain and the Green Knight

One day, King Arthur's court was assembled for a Christmas feast, when a huge green figure rode through the door on a green horse, wielding an axe. He dared the knights to be brave and take a blow at him with his own axe, and he would then return the favour after a year and a day. Gawain decided to shut him up and took the challenge, chopping off the green knight's head it one chop. The giant knight then just picked up his own head and told Sir Gawain to meet him after the allotted time at the Green chapel. He then reattached his head and rode off.

After a time, Sir Gawain set off on his journey. He travelled through the "Wilderness of Wirral" and arrived at a castle, who some believe was Beeston castle in Cheshire. Half dead from the cold, Sir Bercilak and his wife took him in. There was also a hideous old woman who lived there. Sir Bercilak said that the Green chapel was a mere few hours ride away.

Sir Bercilak then announced that he was going hunting in the forest (said to be Delamere). Sir Gawain said he was too tired, so made a deal that he would get any spoils from the hunt in exchange for anything he won in the same period while resting at the castle.

On the first day, Sir Bercilak's wife did her best to seduce Sir Gawain, but he only let her give him one kiss, which he then had to pass onto Sir Bercilak as part of the deal. Over the following two days, this increased to two and then three kisses, which again Sir Gawain passed onto Sir Bercilak. Lady Bercilak then gave Sir Gawain a green sash to protect him from harm, but Sir Gawain did not include this as part of his winnings deal with Sir Bercilak.

The following day Sir Gawain set off for the green chapel. He approached the green knight who was busy sharpening his axe. Sir Gawain kneeled before him waiting for his fate. The green knight went to strike him twice, but did not touch Sir Gawain. Sir Gawain got angry and told him to complete the task. The green knight then took a third blow, but this time just nicked Sir Gawain's neck. The green knight then laughed and revealed that he was actually Sir Bercilak and has been turned into a giant green knight by the hideous old woman at the castle (Morgane in disguise).

Sir Gawain had passed the test, and got a nick just for accepting the sash without declaring it. He rode back to Camelot to tell his story. In honour of Gawain's success, all the knights wore green sashes.

Sir Ro the Cheshire Knight

Sir Ro of Staley Hall (Sir Ralph de Stavelegh) left England to go to fight in the Crusades. Before he left he asked for his wife's wedding ring; he then cut it in half and gave one half back to his wife and kept the other half himself.

Sir Ro was a tough warrior; he fought many battles and had a reputation for being a formidable opponent. Eventually he was captured by the Saracens and was stripped of his armour and dressed in the clothes of a poor man.

He spent months in solitude and began to waste away. Then one night he had a bad dream about an evil threat against his wife that he was powerless to stop. He got down on his knees on the dirty floor of his cell and prayed that he could get home to her, before falling into a gentle sleep.

He woke up blinded by a bright light. When his eyes focussed again, he found himself no longer in the cell, but instead he was in awe to see that he was in the beautiful Cheshire countryside not too far from his home.

He returned to Staley Hall immediately, but was not recognised at the door. He asked the doorman why the flags had changed outside the hall, and was told that the lady of the house was due to marry another the very next day because her husband had been lost during the Crusades. The knight she was due to marry had said that he had been granted the house and lands by the king himself and that the lady was obliged to marry him, even though it was against her will.

Although the dirty and scruffy Sir Ro was not allowed entry to the main building, he was given a meal and drink. He dropped the half gold ring he still had in is possession into his cup and asked a maid to take it to the lady of the house.

When the lady saw the ring, she cried thinking it was from a messenger confirming her husband's demise. She demanded to see the man at once.

She did not recognise the raggedy man as her husband immediately, but then as soon as he spoke her name, she realised who it was. She told him of the lies of the suitor and how he said that she and her people would all be made into beggars if she did not marry him.

Just then the imposter himself arrived and entered the room demanding to know who the scruffy man was embracing his wife-to-be.

The imposter angrily shouted, "What right have you to be here?"

Sir Ro replied, "By the greatest right in the world, the right of master!"

Sir Ro quickly grabbed a mace from the wall and shouted out to the guards. The imposter was caught by the guards, who now recognised their master, and they put the con man into a dungeon for his treachery. Soon after, the imposter was banished from Cheshire for ever on fear of death.

The bells of Staley church rang out upon the news of the return of Sir Ro.

Sir Ro and his lady lived a long and happy life together. At their death they were buried in Mottram Church, where an effigy was placed to their memory above their grave. This effigy can still be seen in the Staley Chapel of the old Church at Mottram.

The Floating Island

Floating on Redesmere near Congleton, there was once an island made of peat.

A young knight was a member of the Capesthorne family. He mistakenly believed his betrothed had been unfaithful to him, and swore he would never look at her face again until the island moved on the water. As soon as he made the accusation he fell seriously ill and had to be nursed by the girl. Meanwhile a huge storm raged outside and tore the island from its roots, blowing it across the mere.

The knight awake from his illness overjoyed that there was a sign of his betroved's virtue and married her immediately, living happily ever after (luckily the girl wasn't one to hold a grudge!).

Lord Percy – Earl of Northumberland

Henry Percy (known as "Hotspur") was a mediaeval English nobleman. He was a valiant knight who captained in the Anglo-Scottish wars (where he earned his nickname). He also led successful rebellions against Henry IV. Lord Percy is immortalised in Shakespeare's play Henry IV part 1.

Percy recruited most of his army from Cheshire; Cheshire bowmen were particularly renowned for their superior abilities and were much better than the king's own bowmen.

Percy was killed at the battle of Shrewsbury in 1403. Henry Percy's body was taken to Whitchurch, Shropshire (close to the Cheshire border) after his death on the battlefield. However, there were lots of rumours that he was still alive, so the king had the corpse exhumed and had it propped up between millstones in the centre of Shrewsbury. The head was then taken and impaled on a gate in York. His four quarters were then taken to London, Newcastle-upon Tyne, Bristol and Chester. Eventually his remains were given back to his widow. This probably proves that even in death, the popular Sir Percy could be a thorn in the king's side for him to have gone to such lengths to prove Percy's death.

Hugh d' Avranches, Earl of Chester (Lupus)

Hugh d'Avranches (1047-1101), also known as *le Gros* and *Lupus*, was the second Norman Earl.

Hugh, due to his gluttony, became so fat that he could hardly walk, earning him the nickname *le Gros* (the fat). He earned his nickname *Lupus* (wolf) because of his ferociousness towards the Welsh. He had palatine powers because of Cheshire's location on the Welsh border.

Hugh spent much of is time fighting with his neighbours in Wales, and with his cousin, Robert of Rhuddlian he subdued a good area of North Wales. He lost Anglesey and much of the rest of Gwynedd in the Welsh revolt of 1094, led by Gruffudd ap Cynan, who had escaped from captivity.

Hugh d'Avranches was said to have sired children to many mistresses, as well as having children with his long suffering wife.

On 23 July 1101, Hugh became a monk and died four days later, being buried in the cemetery of St. Werburgh (his body was later moved). He was succeeded as Earl of Chester by his son Richard, who married Matilda of Blois, a granddaughter of William the Conqueror. Both Richard and Matilda died in the White Ship disaster (1120), and Hugh was then succeeded by his nephew Ranulph le Meschin, Earl of Chester.

Bog Man of Lindow

In August 1984 workmen found the body of a man when they were cutting peat at Lindow Moss near Wilmslow, Cheshire.

The body was not a recent death; the body was from between 2BC – AD 119 (determined by carbon dating). It was taken to the British museum and examined. Due to the conditions in the peat bog, the man's hair, skin and many of his internal organs are still well preserved. He is the most famous preserved man to be found in a UK peat bog.

It is thought that he was not a manual worker because his finger nails were well manicured and his moustache and beard were well trimmed. He died a horrific death after being struck on the top of his head with a heavy object. He also had evidence of a blow to his back that had broken one of his ribs, and also had a cord around his neck. As if that was not enough, he had had his throat cut and was lying face down in the bog. Some people say that it must have been a ritual killing by druids.

He is known as Lindow II (two other bodies have also been found in Lindow moss). He is also known as "Pete Marsh".

The Crosses at Sandbach

The origins of the famous Anglo-Saxon crosses at Sandbach are a source of mystery and legend.

The most commonly told tale is that in the early 9th century, Peada, son of the king of Mercia, fell in love with Alchfleda, daughter of the king of Northumbria. Alchfleda's father would only agree to the marriage if Peada turned to Christianity. Paeda did and then travelled to Northumbria to claim his bride. The crosses are said to commemorate the return of the converted Paeda and his bride. His bride is said to have plotted his death soon afterwards, so it seems it was quite a one-sided relationship!

The crosses stood for nearly a millennia before being broken into pieces in the 17th century and the pieces scatted around, some as far as Oulton Park. In 1816 an historian pieced together as much of the crosses as possible and found some pieces buried, while others were being used as paving stones and porch steps.

The crosses now stand in Sandbach, slightly battered, but more or less in one piece. The crosses now consist of two upright columns set in sockets on a base of three stepped stones. They contain religious carvings, dragons, and strange doll-like heads.

The Seven Sisters Curse

There was once a squire who owned a hall near Dunham Park. He was desperate to have a male heir to inherit the hall. Each time, a daughter was born instead of a son. The squire was angry each time and had a tree planted for each of his daughters to serve as their only inheritance. Seven daughters later, there grew a row of seven trees (the seven sisters). Finally he got a son, but the son was immediately cursed to die by a local wizard, who hated the squire because of the ill-treatment towards his daughters, and wanted to punish him.

The son was quickly sent away abroad to be educated and thinking he had avoided the curse, eventually returned to the hall. His journey was smooth until he reached the seven chestnut trees. As soon as he reached the foot of the trees, a storm began to rage and a bolt of lightning destroyed both him and his carriage and that was the wizard's justice seen through to the end.

Ethelfleda (The Warrior Queen) and the Wedding

The railway bridge in Runcorn was once known as the Ethelfleda bridge. Ethelfleda was a Saxon warrior queen who once lived in a fortress overlooking the river Mersey.

Her father was Alfred the great (who burned the cakes), and even as a young princess, she showed her courage and bravery. Alfred went against his wife's wishes to send Ethelfleda to a convent, and instead trained her alongside her brother to be a warrior – a master of the *seax* (old knife).

Ethelfleda agreed to marry her father's friend, Ethelred; this would unite the kingdoms of the Anglo-Saxons. After the wedding, they rode side by side with their entourage of soldiers, servants, and ladies-in-waiting. However, the Danes were lying in wait for them...

They ambushed the group, Ethelred immediately told his wife and her ladies to flee. Ethelred then faced his enemies and began to fight. However, Ethelfleda turned and saw the battle wasn't going too well, so she turned around with her ladies-in-waiting and joined in the fight. The Danes were taken so by surprise at this attack by the women, and their strength, they then lost the battle. Ethelred looked at his blood-splattered wife and then knew he had a remarkable woman on his hands.

After the battle, they rested at Maiden Castle in Bickerton, where the hill fort gets its name.

Ethrelfleda (The Warrior Queen) and the Siege of Chester

Ingimund led a group of exiled Nordic people desperately trying to find somewhere to settle. They were not welcome in Wales, nor Dublin, so they sailed to the Wirral peninsula. They spoke with Ethrelfleda, who had taken over her elderly husband's affairs, and she said they could settle on the Northern part of the Wirral peninsula out of the way. However, the land was boggy and marshy, with lots of midges; so Ingimund decided that he quite liked the look of Chester instead. There was a meeting of Vikings, and it was decided that they would approach peacefully at first, but then take by force, if required.

The lookouts in Chester saw the band of Vikings approaching the great walled city and panicked. They sent word to Ethelfleda. She sighed when she heard, and had thought they weren't to be trusted. She instructed the people of Chester to open the gates wide as if welcoming them in, then to close behind them to trap them and kill them.

The Vikings walked into the trap, a few died, but a few escaped during the fight, and then went away to make new plans. Igimund was not happy that they had been tricked and put his second plan into action. With helmets on, swords unsheathed and carrying ladders, they marched once again to Chester.

The lookouts saw them again and again asked Ethelfleda for guidance. She sighed and said to collect bricks and rocks together from within the city to throw on the invaders heads. Soon there was a heap of bruised and broken Vikings.

The next plan was to tunnel under the walls to get into the city. Ingimund and his men approached with their digging tools, but were again spotted by the lookouts. The Vikings had shields to protect themselves from the rocks and bricks this time. So next, Ethelfleda instructed the people to take all the ale in the city and boil it up and tip it over the Vikings. Lots of Vikings died that time, boiled by the hot liquid.

The Vikings launched yet another attack, this time with shields and animal hides to protect against stones and hot ale. They continued to dig under the walls. This time a sighing Ethelfleda instructed the people to gather beehives and throw them down onto the Vikings; the little warriors inside would do the job.

The bees stung the Norsemen, and made them retreat back to their marshland on the Wirral. Maybe they might attack again, but certainly not today. Ethelfleda had successfully thwarted their attempts on the city.

The people of Chester went to celebrate, but then realised they had no ale left and they were wondering how they would get their bees back again. A few buildings were missing bricks too...

History and Villains

Vale Royal Abbey

In the heart of Cheshire is an area called Vale Royal. The area was so named because it was popular with royalty who had hunting lodges in the area.

Vale Royal Abbey in Whitegate was founded by the future Edward I, who wanted to make it into the grandest monastery in England. It is said that he made this promise when in danger of being ship wrecked and said he would build it if saved. Monks were moved from nearby Darnhall (an abbey on a Royal estate also founded by Edward).

The abbey did not end up being quite as grand as originally hoped due to numerous issues. Also the monks did not get on very well with their neighbours (putting it lightly!). On several occasions they were attacked by local families who found them to be oppressive landlords. Some monks also were accused of attempted murder themselves. On one occasion a lawless abbot was attacked and killed by a mob (the mob included the vicar of the nearby parish of Over).

After the dissolution of the monasteries, the Holford family took over the abbey (a family related to the Cholmondeleys (pronounced "Chumley")) who were (and still are) major land owners in Cheshire. It was demolished and rebuilt during that time.

The abbey, though changed over the years, still remains in some form as a golf course, wedding venue, and as a set of private apartments. There is a public right of way through the grounds, and you can pass by the abbey from Whitegate village to get to the river Weaver and Vale Royal Locks (Or even as far as the Hartford blue bridge along the old Abbey road). The abbey is also said to have its own ghost in the form of Ida the Nun (there is a circular stone monument marking her grave). There are also rumours of a tunnel that stretches all the way to Knight's Grange (a farm belonging to the monastery about 3 miles away).

Delamere Park

Delamere Park is an affluent private housing estate near Cuddington (and just a short distance from Delamere forest itself). The park has an unusual history with it once being one of the country's largest displacement camps for Polish soldiers following World War II.

The 100 acre site and lodge were owned by the wealthy Wibrahams, who also built Delamere Manor. During World War II, Delamere Park became an army transit camp for British and American soldiers. General George Patton visited "Camp Delamere".

After the war, the disused temporary accommodation was reused for serving Polish soldiers and their families. With Poland under communist control, many Polish people could not return home. Under the Polish resettlement act, the first Polish troops arrived at Delamere in the summer of 1946. At Delamere, many families were reunited after years of separation, but had to share the huts with several other families. The camp came under the jurisdiction of the local authorities and was also used for British families when there a shortage of council owned housing.

Eventually the living conditions were improved, and there was separate accommodation for each family. The two communities co-existed side-by-side.

The Gunpowder Plot and Cheshire

On 5th November every year, people across the UK burn an effigy of Guy (Guido) Fawkes and watch firework displays to remember the failed plot to blow up the House of Lords during the State opening of Parliament on 5th November 1605. The attempt was made to assassinate the king (James I), who was not tolerant towards English Catholics, so that his daughter could be installed as a Catholic head of State.

The plot by Robert Catesby, John Wright, Thomas Wintour, Thomas Percy, Guy Fawkes, Robert Keyes, Thomas Bates, Robert Wintour, Christopher Wright, John Grant, Ambrose Rookwood, Sir Everard Digby and Francis Tresham, was uncovered following an anonymous letter to one of the Lords. Guy Fawkes was found in the cellars guarding 36 barrels of gunpowder (enough to reduce the building to rubble).

So, what is the link to Cheshire? In January 1606, the trial was conducted by Sir Thomas Egerton of Cheshire in his role as Lord High Chancellor. He had come across rebels to the Crown before and had specific (and horrific) ways of extracting confessions using racks and other torture equipment. He got confessions from the surviving plotters and then sentenced them to be hung, drawn and quartered, and made an example of for any future rebels.

The Final Battle of the English Civil War – The Battle of Winnington Bridge

The Battle of Winnington Bridge took place on August 19, 1659 and is widely considered to have been the final battle of the English Civil War.

After the death of Oliver Cromwell in September 1658, his son Richard failed to hold together the Protectorate and Parliament was in conflict with the Army.

A rebellion was planned for August 1, 1659, but many of the various regional groups were not sufficiently well organised and some had been infiltrated by spies.

Sir George Booth, a Royalist supporter, was to command the regional revolt, but received his advice too late. His army of 5,000 had already taken Cheshire before he was informed of the cancelled plan, but he carried on regardless.

John Lambert, said to be Cromwell's cleverest commander, was heading northwards with reinforcements of well trained men. They had passed through Nantwich and camped at Weaverham.

Booth crossed the Weaver to confront Lambert and there was a brief skirmish at Hartford Green. Booth had to retreat across Moss Farm to a stronger position of a long, narrow river bridge backed by a steep slope at Winnington.

Sir George Booth escaped, but a week later a Buckinghamshire innkeeper became suspicious of a Mistress Dorothy, who was accompanied by a large escort of males.

She was reported to the constables as striding like a man and wore large square toed shoes. Next day, more suitably attired, Sir George was on his way to London Tower.

He remained there until February 1660 and with other leaders was released, without ever having been brought to trial.

World War 2 Plane Crash in Hartford, Cheshire

In 1944 a British war plane crashed in the village of Hartford. An account of the event went as follows: The aircraft that crashed in Hartford village was a twin engined Albemarle bomber. It had flown over twice, at very low altitude, skimming the roof tops, in fact, and on the third pass struck the chimney of a house. A Mrs Hodson lived there. One of the crew members was Gerry Crowe who lived a few doors away from Mrs Hodson; he was killed in the crash.

After the aircraft hit a chimney, it then knocked the tops off trees and then came to rest near a wall opposite the village shops. On impact the gun turret catapulted across the main road. A passing American serviceman rescued the gunner, who was badly burned. One of the engines detached and landed inches away from a baby in a pram. The Canadian pilot and the flying officer both died in the crash.

General opinion was that because the wife of one of the crew men lived in Hartford, they were flying low to see her. The plane had travelled from Derbyshire. She insisted that there must just have been engine troubles.

The Last of the Masseys

The Masseys were one of the main land owning families in Cheshire.

The last of the Massey family was William, who decided to become a Jacobite fighting for the invading Scots at the battle of Preston in 1715. He managed to escape the carnage on horseback and made his horse swim across the Mersey and got safe home to Puddington where his horse then died from exhaustion.

He decided to create an alibi by beating up a passing countryman not far from home to try to prove he wasn't at the battle. Unfortunately for him, the man pressed charges and he was immediately arrested. Massey's lies were soon seen though and he was imprisoned at Chester castle. He froze to death in his cell before his case ever went to trial.

Gentleman Edward (the Highwayman) Higgins of Knutsford

There is a plaque in Knutsford for a once famous resident. Highwayman Higgins (or "Squire" Higgins) was a man of good birth and of reasonable means.

He married a wealthy Knutsford woman called Katherine, with whom he had five children. However, he hid a secret that he had previously been convicted of housebreaking in Worcester and had been sentenced to transportation for seven years. While deported to Boston USA, he immediately stole a large amount of money from the house of a rich merchant and bought himself passage home. He lived in Manchester for a short time, before then moving to Knutsford and meeting his wife.

Higgins and his wife socialised with their neighbours, hunting and fishing with them. He also made sure he became familiar with the layout of the houses, just in case he decided to burgle them at some point.

On one occasion Mr and Mrs Higgins were guests of the Egertons, who owned Oulton Park. While playing whist after dinner, Higgins decided to help himself to Mr Egerton's jewelled snuff box lying on the table. He then hid it outdoors for later recovery. In the morning, on the theft being discovered, he earned much approval by summoning all the servants together and having their rooms searched. Mr Egerton was grateful for such prompt action, even though the box was not found.

Another time, Higgins was wandering along the Rows in Chester late at night, when he saw a ladder that a workman had left against the wall of a house in Stanley Street. He climbed up and into a bedroom where a young woman lay asleep. Her jewellery was scattered on the dressing table. Higgins calmly pocketed as much as he could and held his breath when the girl turned over in bed muttering "Oh Mary, please can you put those things straight in the morning", and then made his escape. Years later he admitted he would have had to kill her had she awakened.

He did commit murder on at least one other occasion; he is rumoured to have been involved in the murder of a wealthy woman and her maid in Bristol, so he could steal a hoard of Spanish coins. Apparently, upon his return from Bristol, the neighbourhood as far as Warrington was inundated with foreign gold coins.

There was a notorious stretch of road between Knutsford and Chester that had recently been improved by turn piking (the potholed muddy road had been improved, but travel now meant a toll charge). Traffic on all turnpiked roads was increasing and so therefore were the activities of highwaymen who preyed on the coaches. Higgins found that, with the authorities struggling to do much about the highway robberies, it was good career progression. He "served" as a highwayman along this stretch of road (in between committing the odd burglary here and there).

Eventually, Higgins finally met his end. In 1767, he told his wife he was going out to "collect the rents" and took a journey into Wales, committing a bit of highway robbery along the way. He also decided to do a spot of burglary while he was there and was caught breaking into a house in Carmarthen and was subsequently identified as an escaped prisoner who had defied his deportation years before, and so his fate was sealed. Some tales say he was actually charged for the Spanish coins murder.

On the day of his execution a letter of pardon was sent to the Sheriff of Carmarthen, however it raised suspicion because it had a Brecon postmark as well as a London one and was revealed as an elaborate fake sent out by Higgins himself. Squire Higgins died on the gallows at Carmarthen on 7 November, 1767 and had begged for his wife not to find out the truth of his double life.

His body was sent for medical research, and the mummified body ended up at Owen's College Manchester as a medical teaching aid.

The Murder of the Princes of Wales

Farndon Bridge stands on the border between Cheshire and Wales. It is said to be haunted by the ghosts of two young princes who were murdered there.

The princes were the children of the Welsh prince, Madoc ap Gruffudd. Madoc died in 1236 and had assigned guardians who were tasked with protecting the heirs; these men were John (Earl) Warren and Roger Mortimer. However, they decided it would be much better if they got rid of the heirs instead.

In the middle of the night, the two men travelled from Chester and went to a castle that stood above Llangollen. The two young princes lived in this castle and were removed from their slumber, taken to Farndon Bridge, and then thrown down into the river to drown.

On windy, stormy nights the cries and screams of the young princes, who were killed by the very people set to protect them, are said to be heard from under the bridge.

The Congleton Cannibal

Warning, this story describes dismembered body parts; continue reading at your own risk….

In the 1700s, there was a cannibal on the prowl in Congleton, Cheshire. A ballad singer called Ann Smith had gone missing, and then two boys walking some cows near Astbury, found her cloak with blood stains on it. The police did an extensive search and found more items of clothing, a handbag, and various body parts; including two arms, two legs (severed at the knees), and a breast.

The suspicions fell onto a Congleton butcher's assistant called Samuel Thorley. He also worked part time as a grave digger and was a big man with a foul temper. A widow who housed Thorley contested that she had seen Thorley eating some strange looking meat, which he claimed was just some pork. A local surgeon was given a sample of some of the left over meat and it was identified as actually being human flesh.

Thorley was hanged in 1777 and a month later his body suspended from a gibbet. Nobody ever found out what drove him to kill and eat parts of his victim.

The Deadly Duel and Church Minshull

The pretty village of Church Minshull has a monument to a famous duel that took place. It is said to be the only duel in English history where both people died.

The story starts in Gawsworth where Sir Edward Fitton died leaving his fortune to his only daughter, who had died before him. His two sisters then tried to lay claim to his estate. There were law suits, fraudulent wills, and quarrels that lasted for years. It eventually came to a head when Lord Mohun and the Duke of Hamilton decided to meet at a park in London and have a duel on behalf of the two sisters.

Following the simultaneous deaths during the duel, a monument was set up by the family of Thomas Minshull (whose mother was one of the sisters), proclaiming the wrongdoings to that sister in the whole affair.

Tatton Park

Tatton Park is a historic estate in Cheshire, England, to the north of the town of Knutsford. It contains a mansion, Tatton Hall, a manor house dating from medieval times, Tatton Old Hall, gardens, a farm and a deer park of 2,000 acres (8.1 km^2). It is now a popular visitor attraction.

There is evidence of human habitation going back to the Iron Age. In medieval times the village of Tatton was on the site. This has since disappeared but the area of the village and its roadways are a Scheduled Ancient Monument.

For nearly 400 years the estate was the property of the Egerton family (until 1958). During World War II Lord Egerton's parkland played a major role in the training of all allied paratroops with a Parachute training school. Between 1940 and early 1946, approximately 60,000 trainees from the United Kingdom and several European countries, made their first training drops from cages suspended from Barrage balloons over an open area to the northwest of the hall.

Deer at Tatton Park

Crewe Lyceum, the Railway and the Great Train Robbers

Crewe is probably best known for its extensive railway station and its long history of railway works in the town. It was also the home of Rolls Royce for about 60 years, and is still home to Bentley. The modern urban settlement of Crewe was formally planned out in 1843 to consolidate the "railway colony". Until the Grand Junction Railway (GJR) company chose Crewe as the site for its locomotive works and railway station, Crewe was a village with a population (c. 1831) of just 70 residents.

Despite Crewe town being relatively new, there are still rumours of resident ghosts; including the ghost of a murdered thespian which is said to haunt the Lyceum theatre in the town centre. While the ghost of a ballet dancer dressed in white, who took her own life, is said to dance on the stage there. She leaves a strong perfume scent behind when she is seen. An exorcism took place in 1969, but people have claimed to have seen the ghosts since then.

Crewe, with its railways, also has connections to the infamous "Great train robbery". Far from being a glamorous likeable villain story as often portrayed in films and books, the fact is it was a very violent crime; two men from Crewe suffered long-term trauma from the events, and both died within 9 years of the incident. The driver of the train, Jack Mills, suffered severe injuries from being clubbed over the head with an axe handle, from which he never fully recovered. His fellow cab member, David Whitby, died of a heart attack at just 34 years old. The people of Crewe still remember and commemorate their townsmen who suffered in this robbery.

Cheshire Minstrels

The origin of the Cheshire minstrels is said to come from an event that happened at a midsummer fair.

Sir Ranulph de Blunderville, Earl of Chester, was besieged in his castle at Ruddlian in Wales, so John Lacey, constable of Cheshire, aided by certain minstrels from the fair, collected together a great number of disorderly people and sent them to help the Earl. The Welsh, seeing their numbers, and not realising that they weren't actually armed, immediately backed down and called off the siege.

This led to the tradition where the minstrels had a procession on midsummer's day with the Lord of Dutton. This tradition continued until 1756. It has recently started again with a band of present day minstrels.

The Trap and the Kidnapped Mayor

In 15th century Chester, there were border disputes between the English and the Welsh.

The Mayor of Chester banned Welsh people from the streets of his city after sunset (and set the law about it being legal to shoot a Welshman within the city walls). One man, Reinallt took offense to this and sought revenge.

He kidnapped the Mayor during the Chester fair and took him back to his castle in Mold, Clwyd, with two hundred soldiers from Chester in close pursuit. The soldiers forced their way into the castle and were confronted with the dead body of the Mayor, before realising it was a trap. Reinallt's men closed the gates behind them and then set fire to the whole castle, killing all inside. The feud continued for many years after.

The Old Whitegate Pub

Whitegate village is near to Vale Royal Abbey and is situated between Northwich and Winsford. There is a thatched cottage in the centre of the Cheshire village of Whitegate, at the junction just near the church. Long ago this was a popular pub used by all the locals.

However, Lady Delamere, of Vale Royal Abbey, decided to close it down and have it turned into a house because she objected to people going there straight after church and getting drunk.

That part of the village has changed little in the last couple of hundred years.

Ghosts and ghostly goings on

Haunted Stile of Macclesfield

There is a place called Gun Hill near Macclesfield that was once used for public executions. In 1731 a man named John Naden was strung up on the gibbet (a gallows-type structure) for killing his employer. He has been paid to do so by his employer's wife, but had to get so drunk to do it that while rifling through the dead man's pockets to make it look like a robbery, he accidentally left his knife under the body and was therefore convicted of the crime and sentenced to death.

The gibbet stood until the 1880s and the wood was then used to make a stile at the edge of the field. The stile is said to be haunted by the ghost of John Naden and other souls who had died on the gibbet. John himself is said to be very unfriendly and drunk, so if you get a whiff of spirits next time you climb over a stile near Macclesfield, it may be a spirit in more ways than one....

The ghost of the Roman Soldier

Chester is an old Roman fortified city. The ghost of a fallen Roman soldier is said to pace endlessly between the amphitheatre and the ruined Roman tower beside Newgate (in the city walls).

The ghost is said to be that of a decurion of the XI Legion Adriutix and lived in Chester soon after the Roman conquest.

The decurion fell in love with a local girl and would slip out of the fortress city to meet with her. Unfortunately for him, a local band of Celtic warriors found out and one day followed the girl as she went to meet the Roman.

As soon as they spotted the decurion, the warriors ambushed him and bundled him into a ditch. They then slipped into the city through the open gate to steal and plunder as much as they could. The decurion managed to get out of the ditch and rushed to raise the alarm, but was cut down by a Celtic sword.

The route taken by the spirit is said to be the route he would needed to have taken to warn his comrades or according to other sources, it is the route he took as part of his guard duties.

Ghostly Horsemen

A shadowy figure of a man on horseback is said to cross a lane in Bunbury, Cheshire. Another with a horse and cart has been seen near the forest train station at Delamere.

There is also a story of a horseman who visited Bramhall Hall one stormy night on New Years Eve 1630. He was dressed in red from head to foot and had a red cloak over his shoulders. His steed was huge and was coal black in colour. Although the mysterious horseman was a stranger and had a cold sinister appearance, he was given food and wine and was given a room to sleep in.

The next morning, the knight who owned the hall was found stone dead on the floor of his bedroom and the mysterious horseman had disappeared. The ghost of the horseman and his steed is said to gallop into the courtyard of the hall every New Years Eve.

The Weeing Ghosts of Warrington

In the 1970s there was a strange occurrence that happened seven days in a row inside a shop that had been built out of a converted school in Warrington. The building kept getting urine puddles on the floor that would dry up and leave white stains.

The building was securely locked, so there was no evidence that animals or teenagers were getting in, or a leaky roof, but every morning the puddles would re-appear.

On one of the days a witness saw an arc of urine appearing in midair from about 18 inches high and pouring onto the floor.

One religious customer began to pray that the ghosts would go and then woke up the next day to find her bed had been soaked through with urine.

Nobody knows why it suddenly stopped after seven days, or why the mischievous ghosts wanted to wee there, but they never came back again.

Spectral Hounds and Big Cats of Cheshire

There are several accounts of spectral hounds, or ghost dogs, at various locations around Cheshire.

One account talks of a fishmonger from Hyde who was walking along a lane in Godley Green, when a tan coloured dog as big as a large horse starting walking beside him. The man tried to run, but the dog kept up. He then tried to punch it to scare it away, but his fist went straight through the dog's head and hit the bush behind. The ghost dog didn't seem to be angered by this and carried on following him. The fishmonger finally fled and managed to escape it. The man said there had been a horrible clanging sound like chains dragging during the ordeal. A little girl had seen something similar in the same area several years before, and also in that case, the dog was not aggressive towards her. Locals have speculated that it is a kind of "guide" dog trying to lead people somewhere or guard them.

In another event involving a spectral hound, a black dog was seen galloping down a road at Barthomley Rectory, another haunts the gates of Spurstow Hall, and a white dog dragging chains has been seen near a school in Bunbury.

All these accounts of dogs involve ghosts, but there have also been huge cats seen in the area that are very much alive. In August 1980 a farmer reported seeing a cat as large as an alsation dog, but with a cat's head and tail. In 1976, in Upton near Chester, a huge cat similar to a lioness was spotted wandering around the area. Chester zoo, which is in that area, had no lionesses or similar large cats missing. Could there be a special breed of giant Cheshire cats roaming around the Cheshire countryside?

The lady ghosts of Marbury Hall

There was once a hall at Marbury Park near Northwich (demolished in 1968). It was said to be home to five lady ghosts. Some sources seem to merge some of these ladies together to be one or two people, but it seems that they are actually five separate people, each with their own story.

The first is the ghost of Lady Barrymore. She is said to have received a mare as a wedding present, which, due to a bet made by Lord Barrymore, was sent on an epic run from sunrise to sunset. The lady waited anxiously for her return, and finally saw the mare come running with bloody foam coming out of her mouth. The mare was led to the well for a drink, but then collapsed and died. The lady was heart broken and died of grief. Her dying wish was that she wanted to be buried by the well where her treasured mare had died. However, Lord Barrymore ignored her wishes and buried her body in the churchyard. A few days later he found the spirit of his wife by the well asking over an over why he had ignored her wishes and that she would ride her beloved mare for ever. It is said that at sunset the lady can sometimes be seen riding her ghost horse through the dusk.

A gravestone is said to lie within the park:

HERE LIES THE MARBURY DUNNE
THE FASTEST HORSE THAT EVER RUN
CLOTHED IN A LINEN SHEET
WITH SILVER SHOES UPON HER FEET

The second, an English lady, one of the Smith-Barry's, was murdered on the 7th step on the main staircase. The blood stain would never go away. When the hall was being rebuilt, bones were found near the staircase.

The third is one Lady Smith-Barry who was having an affair. Her husband followed her one night and murdered her. It is said she met her lover in one of the tunnels under the hall; which was where her ghost resided. Some tunnels are still said to exist underground within the park.

The fourth, Miss Alice Knappett loved Marbury Hall. She was the Head Housemaid at the turn of the 20th century. She was a matronly figure who rode her bike on the grounds. Her spirit is known as the lady in Black.

The fifth is another lady ghost (the white lady). She was an Egyptian woman who had fallen in love with a man called John Hugh Smith-Barry (1748-1801) and had followed him home after he met her on his travels. He was already married so hid her identity by employing her as a maid so he could continue their affair. One day she "accidentally" fell down the stairs and died. She had apparently said that if she ever died she wanted to be kept in the hallway, so her body was embalmed and kept in a coffin in the entrance hall, but her ghost would walk continuously through the house. They moved her to the family vault in Great Budworth, but she continued to haunt the house and then started also ringing bells. Then her body was dumped into Budworth mere. This time the hauntings reached an unprecedented scale. They finally retrieved the body and buried it in the rose garden next to the house, and the hauntings finally ceased.

The Headless Woman of Tarvin

The family who owned Hockenhull Hall in Tarvin were staunch royalists. During the civil war (in about 1664) the family escaped, but their maid (Grace Trigg) was found hiding in a cellar, and was captured by Cromwell's troops.

Grace refused to talk, even under torture. Eventually the troops gave up and struck off her head with a sword. It is said that she was killed in the attic of a local inn, and then her body was dumped over the side of one of two "Roman Bridges" (medieval packhorse bridge), one of which is still standing.

Legend says that 250 years after her beheading, the owners of the inn found bloodstains still remaining in the attic. Her ghost has been reported to walk around Tarvin and Duddon, visiting local parks and bridges with the head being carried under the arm.

She is also said to carry her head to the inn where she died, which is now called...The Headless woman.

There are also tales of a second headless woman in the area called Dorothy who died at around the same time. Somehow her head was chopped off by her own father as he tried to protect her from Cromwell's troops.

The Gately Groaner

Jim Barrow wan a bad tempered and mean man. He was a blatant con man who watered down the milk he sold and was disliked by all the locals.

When he died, people were glad. He is said to have been a nuisance after death. His spirit was said to have kept rising from his grave and he would moan and groan his way up and down the lane.

The locals had had enough and called in the local clergymen. They had to wait for him to start walking, and then block him by surrounding him as they carried lit candles. They cornered him and drew a circle around him while praying. That was said to have blocked him and Jim Barrow was finally silenced.

The Chester Leyline

Leylines are said to be invisible energy lines that intersect the earth and join aligned points of special interest (for example, one crosses through Stone Henge, and another through the great pyramids of Egypt). Leylines are often paths of importance walked by many people over many years. They are also said to be where spirits are most likely to be. In Chester a leyline is said to run through the middle of the city, from St Werburgh Street to the cathedral.

There are said to be lots of spirits within Chester, which is no surprise being a city with 2000 years of history. When the Romans left Chester, there were successive waves of Celts, Vikings, Saxons and Normans. Edward I kept armies there to fight the Welsh, and Royalist cavaliers defended the walled city against Parliamentarians.

The rumoured spirits include a Roman soldier and Billy Hobby the. There is also a cavalier, a woman called "Henrietta" whose lover was another Cavalier killed in battle (she looks out of a window waiting for her love to return), there is also a horseman, and lots of other ghosts and ghouls. There is an official Chester ghost tour that you can take around the city hotspots.

The Headless Duck

There are numerous ghost animals reported around Cheshire, but perhaps the most unusual one is the ghost one is the ghost of a duck in Stanney. The ghost of a duck suddenly appeared in a lane and would peck at passing ankles.

The village parson tried to exorcise it, but to no avail, so the local butcher went with his cleaver and chopped the ghosts head off and dumped the head in a ditch. The lane is still haunted, but now with a headless duck.

The Real and Fake Ghosts of Davenham

Leftwich Hall was haunted by a spirit known as the Crowton Grey Lady. It would be seen drifting through the rooms and would then stop on one particular section of wall. Eventually the wall was torn down and there was a woman's skeleton inside. This was then buried in Davenham graveyard and the spirit was never seen again.

Also in Davenham, a small bridge on the path between Shipbrook and Whatcroft was said to have a ghost that haunted it. Local residents were terrified by a dancing coffin with an eerily glowing skeleton inside. It eventually turned out to be an elaborate prop set up by local poachers to keep people away from the area, and also to act as an alarm for them that someone was approaching and disturbing their poaching activities.

The Ghost in a Bottle

There has been the tale of a headless ghost duck that haunted a lane in Cheshire. There was also another ghost duck that haunted a pub.

The landlord of the Blue Bell Inn in Tushingham had a cute fluffy duckling that would walk around the bar. However it grew up to be a vicious duck after getting fed up of having beer slopped on it, smoke blown onto it and get accidentally kicked one to many times. It would waddle around and peck all the customers. Reluctantly the landlord had to kill it. He buried its body under the bottom step of the cellar.

However, soon after that, the step kept coming loose and the ghost of the duck would emerge and start pecking away at people's ankles. The landlord went to the local vicar to arrange an exorcism. It took all the parsons in the area, and during the procedure the ghost began to shrink, so the local vicar grabbed a bottle, put the duck inside and quickly corked it up. The bottle was then bricked up inside the wall of the cellar.

Quite recently, when the pub was undergoing repairs, the sealed bottle was found. It was quickly put back inside a new wall. The owners didn't want to take any chances!

The Ghost of Anne Boleyn

There are conflicted tales as to Anne Boleyn's birthplace, but local Cheshire legend says that the infamous lady was born in Bollin Hall, Cheshire.

As most people know, she was the second wife of Henry VIII and was beheaded. Her ghost is said to haunt Bollin Hall among other places (also the Tower of London, Hampton Court place and Blickling Hall).

River Ghost of Chester

We have mentioned some of the many ghosts of Chester. There is another that is more mysterious than all the rest and is said to have been spotted by numerous witnesses.

The witnesses report seeing a dark misty, shifty figure that wreathes and writhes out of the dark water of the canal near Griffith's old flour mill and spreads itself on the tow path, as if waiting for prey.

Boggarts of Cheshire

Boggarts can appear in many forms; human, animal, skeletal or goblin-like. They can be kindly or malicious.

A farm labourer was walking between Frandley and Barnton in Cheshire, an as he reached Dog Kennel wood he met a man who was four feet tall. The man moved to let him past and then stood by a stile. As the labourer turned to see, he saw the man grow larger and larger until he was giant sized. The labourer ran away as fast as he could, and was convinced it was a boggart.

Stiles and gates were said to be popular haunts of boggarts in Cheshire. One was said to haunt a gate in Tattenhall.

The Unfillable Hole

In 1823 a man called William Wood was attacked by robbers on the road between Disley and Whaley. His head was smashed hard into the ground by the savagery of the attack. Two of the three outlaws escaped, but one was caught and hanged.

In the spot where William's head was pushed into the ground remained a hollow where no grass would grow. Nothing could fill it in either.

In 1859 a man tried to fill it multiple times with stones, only to find the stones scattered around the next day. Someone else years later also tried to fill the hole and cover it with earth, but it also was rejected from the hole and the content flung all around.

Little Moreton Hall Ghostly Goings On

Little Moreton Hall near Congleton is a Tudor house, dating back to the 15th century. The property has a moat that goes around it, and there is a very old knot garden outside.

Following the Black Death, the Moreton family bought up land in the area. Over generations, they extended and added to the house. The family were staunch Royalists in what became a Parliamentarian area and weren't always very popular.

There is a mound outside the house and there are rumours that there was once a secret tunnel from the house to it. Some people think that there is confusion between a rumoured tunnel and the leyline that is said to run through the grounds.

There is said to be the ghost of a grey lady in the long gallery. She drifts along and then disappears. In the chapel there the sound of a sobbing child is often heard. A few years ago, a teenage girl visiting the National Trust property reported seeing an evil face appear in one of the fireplaces, and then disappear again after a few seconds.

On the A34 road that runs nearby, there were numerous reports of strange figures appearing on the road and nearly causing accidents for passing motorists (in 2000-2002). The police investigated to see who the people were that were walking along that road, and were confronted with a ghostly horse drawn carriage that sped past and then disappeared as it turned into the driveway of Little Moreton Hall….

Maggoty Johnson

This a tale of a ghost who is creepier than any of the ghosts of Cheshire described previously. This is the tale of a ghost jester called Maggoty Johnson.

Samuel "maggoty" Johnson was an 18th century playwright, comedian, and dancing master (the word "maggoty" means that someone is odd and is said to have maggots in the brain). Maggoty played for guests at Gawsworth Hall and other surrounding halls; he was very a very popular act.

His last dying wish was to be buried in unconsecrated ground (it is believed it was to challenge the popular belief that people who did that would return as a ghost). However, it seems that his ghost did then actually appear; there are tales of a ghostly shape of a man, with tight trousers and a hat with bells on it, in a wood known as Maggoty's wood.

One dark winter's night, a man saw a figure dancing in the woods in the snow and at first thought it must be a drunk, except when he approached the figure he disappeared and the dancing man had left no footsteps whatsoever in the snow.

Another time a man was driving along the road that runs parallel to Maggoty's wood, when a figure jumped at of nowhere. The driver slammed on his brakes, but could not stop in time and the car ploughed right into the shape. The driver said the windscreen went black as if a sheet had fallen onto it. When he came to a stop, the frightened driver jumped out of his car, but there was nobody there…

Beware if you ever decide to walk or drive near to Maggoty's wood, otherwise you may just see old Maggoty himself.

The Ghostly Raven of Coppenhall

During the First World War, a young soldier from Coppenhall was drowned at sea. Shortly afterwards his mother was found drowned in a horse trough. Thereafter a raven (who locals believed to be the mother's ghost) was seen frequently perched on the rim of the trough.

A local grocer dismissed the story of the raven being the mother and openly laughed about it until he too was found drowned in the same trough.

The raven was said to have haunted the area for some time later, until an exorcism was carried out. The raven has not been seen since.

Old Laws, Cures and Customs

Strange old law of Chester

Chester (Deva) was founded 2000 years ago as one of the three main Roman legionary fortresses (the others were York and Caerleon). The ancient walled city, with its amphitheatre, remains of Roman hypocaust systems and remains of ancient buildings.

The Rows of Chester are unique within Britain, with shops and dwellings across two floors with the ground floor often lower than the street level.

Perhaps one of the most unusual facts about Chester is a law (that still stands) that says that you can legally shoot a Welsh person with a bow and arrow inside the city walls as long as it is after midnight...

Wedding Ropes

In Cheshire and some other counties bordering Wales, there was a tradition after a wedding that the porch, path, or even public road outside would be "roped" against the wedding party by villagers.

They would not remove the obstacle until the bridegroom had distributed money to them. Sometimes the rope would have flowers tied to them, which the bridal party would have to "pay" for.

Old Cures and Customs of Cheshire

There are lots of strange old customs that at one time were regularly undertaken within Cheshire. Here are just a few of them:

- Feeding a sow toast with lots of lard on would apparently prevent her from eating her own piglets.
- Rubbing a wart on a piece of meat and then burying the meat until it rots was said to cure the wart.
- Sewing the shoulder bone of a rabbit into a cloth and carrying it around would cure rheumatism.
- To cure whooping cough, people would find a briar bush with an arched branch and pass the child underneath.
- To cure earache, the patient held a roasted onion against the affected ear for as long as they could.
- Woodlice were used as tablets for a range of illnesses.
- Roasted mouse pie was eaten to cure insomnia.
- To cure a bad cough, people would put a live frog in their mouth. One woman complained that her son had virtually sucked two toads dry and it hadn't worked.
- To cure toothache, people would find a tooth from a churchyard and wear it around the neck.
- The right hand of a hanged criminal was known as a "hand of glory". If chopped off, dried and turned into a candlestick, and then held (with the candle lit) while saying a particular rhyme, it could apparently open any locked door. The only way to destroy the effects of a "hand of glory" was to distinguish the flame with milk.

- The healing well of Delamere (fed by a special spring) and a similar well at Spurstow were said to cure a variety of illnesses.

May Day in Cheshire

Like the rest of Britain, May Day is celebrated in Cheshire. There is a celebration in Knutsford that has been going since 1864. At one times there would be precessions with character such as Maid Marion and Robin Hood, Morris Dancers, and the Queen of May, also in honour of the author Elizabeth Gaskell (a Knutsford resident), an ancient Sedan chair.

There is a legend that the king of Canute (aka Knut) came to Knutsford and built a ford; this gave the town its name. It is said he got sand in his shoes, so there has been a tradition of throwing sand at Knutsford weddings.

Another Cheshire May Day tradition (popular during the 1920s and 1930s) is to carry staves decorated with wooden oak apples, if you gave up before noon then you would be stung with nettles.

In the 19th century in Cheshire, some secretive people called May birchers would sneak to houses on May eve and put a branch of a tree or shrub on the doorstep to be found the next morning. There was a secret code: nut for a slut, pear if you're fair, plum if you're glum, bramble if you ramble, alder (pronounced 'owler') if you're a scowler, and gorse for the whores.

Riding the Stang

If a couple were having lots of public quarrels, then straw-stuffed effigies were made of the couple and then tied to long poles (stangs). This would be carried through the jeering crowds to the offending couple's house with the crowd following, making as much noise as possible. The effigies would then be burned on a bonfire in view of the couple's window.

It has variations, with one couple's effigy being tied back to front onto a donkey.

The author, Elizabeth Gaskell, once wrote about the "Riding the Stang" custom being commonplace all over Cheshire; if a woman had regularly scolded her husband in public, then the woman herself would be forced to sit backwards on an old shabby horse and would be forced to parade through the town, followed by people beating pots and pans.

Paternal Madness

In the 1890s there was a case of a man going temporarily mad during his wife's pregnancy. Cheshire folklore took it to mean that the child would be a boy – it was. The man was said to have recovered afterwards.

Healing Well of Delamere

In 1600 a leaflet was published in London about a "newe found well" in Delamere, Cheshire that could cure a wide variety of ailments. The well sat at the foot of a holly tree in the forest. Numerous visitors bathed and drank the water and it was said that it cured blindness, ruptures, deafness, lameness and gout.

One man was rumoured to have turned up there barely able to walk, then after bathing in the water he strode off flinging his crutches into a nearby tree. Centuries before that discovery, there had been a myth of a well in the forest called St Stephen's well; it is likely they were one and the same. Who knows if the healing well still exists somewhere in Delamere forest, and if the mystery of the supposed healing powers will ever be revealed?

Blakemere moss, Delamere

Creatures of Cheshire

The Singing Mermaid of Blackrock

Long ago there were tales of a mermaid who lived just off the north Wirral coast near to Leasowe castle. She would sit at midnight and would sing and comb her hair. She was said to be both irresistible and deadly to young men.

A sailor called John Robinson was the last survivor of a crew of men who had been out in their ship in a huge storm. He found the mermaid and invited her on board his ship. By being the first to speak and taking her comb and girdle, he was allowed a wish and said he wanted to meet her again the following Friday. She, in return, gave him a compass to allow him to return to shore.

The next time they met, she spoke first and therefore had power over him. She bewitched him with her singing, took back the compass and gave him her ring as a keepsake, saying she would soon see him again. This time, however, he returned home and immediately fell ill. He died exactly 5 days later.

There are rocks near Leasowe castle called the Mermaid Stones. If you happen to hear some strange singing if you are ever there, make sure you run away lest the same fate befalls you.

Nellie Longarms

There is a tale of a creature at Wybunbury moss called Nellie Longarms. For generations, tales have been told that Nellie will pull people into the murky depths of the bog with her long arms if you get too close to the edge.

Wybunbury moss has a floating raft of moss. The tale was probably a way of warning children to keep away from the water because of the floating moss and the duck weed that can wrap itself around your legs.

This water spirit has also been known as Ginny Greenteeth, Jeannie Greenteeth, Wicked Jenny and Peg O'Nell.

The Dragon of Moston

In around the 12th century, the village of Moston in Cheshire was being terrorised by a terrifying dragon with triple rows of fangs, flaming eyes, a scaly body, and huge claws.

A man called Thomas Venables (descendant of Sir Gilbert Venables, commissioner to William the Conqueror) decided to take on the beast and put an end to its rampage.

Venables went to look for the dragon on a lane between Sandbach and Middlewich. When he found the dragon, it had just finished devouring a small child that it had seized. Thomas began to battle the dragon and firstly wounded it with arrows. One arrow got stuck in the dragon's eye, blinding it on one side. Thomas took his chance and leapt around to the blind side of the dragon, he then finished off the beast with his sword.

Thomas was given the manor of Moston as a reward, and the Venables family coat of arms now shows a dragon with an arrow in its eye. The coat of arms is carved on a screen in the Venable's chapel of Middlewich church. The lake in the field where the fight took place is now called Dragon's lake and lane it is along is called Dragon's Lane.

The Giant of Hale

A man called John Middleton was born in the village of Hale, in Cheshire (the Hale that is close to Liverpool). He was said to be 9 feet 3 inches tall (2.81 m).

Due to his stature, he was hired by the sheriff of Lancashire as a bodyguard. He was so tall that he had to sleep at night with his feet sticking out of the window of his small house.

One day he went down to London to have a wrestling match against the king's champion wrestler. John the giant beat the king's champion and managed to break his thumb. The king was embarrassed and annoyed that many of his subject had lost their bets on the match, so he sent John back home with the princely sum of £20 (a lot of money in those days). However, on his journey back up from London, he was mugged by his jealous companions who took advantage of his apparently slow wits. John returned to Hale penniless, where he stayed until he died.

He is buried in the church yard in Hale and there is a life-sized statue of him across from the church; the inscription reads "Here lyeth the body of John Middleton the Childe Nine feet three Borne 1578 Dyede 1623". He is now known as the "Childe of Hale".

The Asrai

One clear moonlit night, a man was out on his boat fishing in one of Cheshire's deep meres, when he caught something heavy in his fishing net.

He opened his net and found a beautiful young girl, no larger than a twelve year old child; she had long green hair and webbed fingers and toes.

The fisherman then remembered tales of a race of shy, gentle water spirits called the Asrai, who inhabited the deepest lakes in Cheshire and Shropshire. They grew by the light of the moon and only surfaced once a century.

The creature was struggling to get free and kept pointing up at the moon, which was now setting. Her speech was soft, like ripples in the water, but he could not understand what she was trying to tell him.

Although he felt guilty about her distress, he still decided he wanted to take her home to show to his children. He also thought he might get some money if he could sell her as an exhibit.

The Asrai seemed to guess his intentions and put her webbed hand on to his arm to plead to him. Her touch was so cold that it left a red mark on him. The touch also hurt her and she curled up weeping.

The fisherman then remembered how the Asrai were afraid of daylight, so he covered her with rushes in his boat and rowed to shore. When he arrived at the jetty in the daylight and pulled back the rushes, there was just a pool of water. The only thing he had left from the encounter was the mark that was still on his arm from her touch.

Lines taken from *The Asrai (Prologue To The Changeling.)* by Robert Buchanan

'Before man grew of the four elements,
The Asrai grew of three—fire, water, air—
Not earth,—they were not earthly. That was ere
The opening of the golden eye of day:
The world was silvern,—moonlight mystical
Flooded her silent continents and seas,—
And in green places the pale Asrai walked
To deep and melancholy melody,
Musing, and cast no shades.
'These could not die
As men die; Death came later; pale yet fair,
Pensive yet happy, in the lonely light
The Asrai wander'd, choosing for their homes
All gentle places—valleys mossy deep,
Star-haunted waters, yellow strips of sand
Kissing the sad edge of the shimmering sea,
And porphyry caverns in the gaunt hillsides,
Frosted with gems and dripping diamond dews
In mossy basins where the water black
Bubbled with wondrous breath.

The Changeling of Mottram

WARNING: This story is a bit gruesome, so if you happen to be a small child, or have a nervous disposition, do not read any further! Actually some small children will probably like this story!

In the 17th century a man was hanged for stealing deer. The wife had begged to the steward for clemency, but it was in vain. After the execution, she stayed by the hanging body of her husband, clutching their newborn baby. A while later, an old witch appeared; she had come to remove the fat from the body for use in her spells. Strangely the widow and the witch became friends and kept a vigil by the body trying to ward off scavenging crows. During this vigil, lasting days, the widow's baby died.

The witch then hatched a plan with the widow. The old witch crept into the steward's house and stole the baby that had just been born to the steward's wife. She then put the body of the dead baby in an obvious place, in a clearing in some nearby woodland, where its face was eaten away by rats and became unrecognisable. The tearful steward came across the body during the search for his missing infant and naturally assumed it was his baby.

The steward's real baby was brought up by the widow and witch in the widow's small cottage nearby. In time, the boy was taught to be a thief and a poacher; he was especially encouraged to steal from the steward. Until one day, the witch betrayed the young man to the steward, who was promptly arrested by the steward and sentenced to hanging. At the foot of the gallows, the widow and the witch laughed strangely throughout the proceedings.

As soon as the young man was dead, the witch and the widow revealed to the steward that the man he had just killed was actually his own son. Horrified the Steward collapsed, the widow took poison, and the witch was never seen again.

The Mermaid and the Bell

Previously mentioned, the tale of the singing mermaid has been told. Some say there were multiple mermaids, but some believe that the same mermaid swam in an underground tunnel to Rostherne Mere.

In this story, the mermaid lived in a stretch of water that ran from Alderley to High Legh; Rostherne Mere was part of it.

Every year on Easter Sunday the mermaid would appear at dawn and ring a sunken bell (from Rostherne church; it was said to have accidentally rolled into the water and had sunk into the depths). The mermaid would also sit on the bell and sing.

The Blacksmith Who Killed A Griffin

There was a brave hero who lived near Widnes. This hero wasn't a knight, he was just an ordinary townsman who took on a fearsome griffin.

Farnworth is a village that now forms part of Widnes. There is a legend of a griffin that was terrorising the people of the area and killing livestock. Everyone in the village persuaded the toughest man in the village, the local blacksmith, to fight the griffin.

The blacksmith fought a long battle against it and finally killed it. He was proclaimed a hero by the other villagers and became known as "the bold", his surname then became "Bold" and the Griffin appears on the family's heraldic decorations.

The Doctor and the Devil

A doctor in Longendale made a deal with the devil to have his soul. When his time was up, he arrived at the meeting place on horseback. The devil was already on horseback, so the doctor persuaded the devil to race him for his soul.

The devil liked games, so gave the doctor a head start, but soon caught up and started twirling the doctor's horse's tail in amusement. The horse was not too impressed with this, and in fear leaped into a nearby stream. The devil could not cross running water and tried to pull the horse back, but ended up with just its detached tail in his hand.

The old Roman road where this was said to have taken pace is now known as "The Doctor's road".

The Devil and the Church

Over church (St Chads) was said to have once stood in the middle of the town near to where Over Square is now (Winsford, Cheshire). One day the devil decided to pick up the entire church and fly away with it; apparently annoyed that the people of Over refused to worship him.

Some say it was the monks of Vale Royal Abbey ringing their bells, some say it was the people of Over praying, or the combination of both, but whichever theory, the church was dropped safely by the devil at its current site, a mile from town down a quiet lane.

Billy Hobby's Well, Chester

Grosvenor Park in Chester was developed on land given to the city of Chester by Richard Grosvenor (2nd Marques of Westminster) in the 1860s.

There was a field called Billie Hobby's field on this land and it was said to be magic; young women would go and stand on their right leg in the field and wish for husbands. The original well in the field had a canopy built over it as part of the redevelopment. The rest of the field was developed into the park.

Some say that Billy Hobby himself is a mischievous goblin who lives around this part of the park (probably laughing at all the women standing on one leg!).

Prince Henry and the Werewolf

During the reign of Henry II, villagers in Longendale appealed for help to the Abbot of Basingwerke because they were being terrorized by a ravaging werewolf. The abbot put a curse that the werewolf would have to stay in its animal form, and then sent out a hunting party.

The king's son, Prince Henry, was part of the hunt, but became separated from the rest of the group. He was then suddenly ambushed by the werewolf itself. The Prince quickly turned and plunged his spear deep into the creature's side. The creature cried out a cry of pain in a human voice. It then attacked the Prince again and was about to kill him when another member of the hunting party appeared and quickly slayed the werewolf.

Inside the werewolf's stomach they found the head of three babies it had eaten that morning. A forester came forward and said he had seen the wolf trying to rip its own fur, just before the hunt, as if wanted to get rid of it and maybe change back to human form. It had the voice of a woman. The identity of the person itself had been was never discovered.

All the rest

Jodrell Bank

Jodrell Bank Centre for Astrophysics (the UK national centre) hosts a number of radio telescopes, with the main one being the huge Lovell telescope (a famous landmark in the east of the County).

The telescopes are used for researching cosmic rays, meteors, quasars, pulsars, masers and gravitational lenses.

There is also the MERLIN array of dishes around the country (MERLIN stands for Multi-Element Radio Linked Interferometer Network), with the hub being at Jodrell Bank. Four of the seven dishes in the array are in Cheshire, with two at Jodrell (one being the Lovell telescope itself), one at Darnhall and one at Pickmere.

The visitor centre at Jodrell Bank has been revamped and has lots of information about meteorites black holes, and general cool space information.

Salt in Cheshire

Cheshire is famous for its salt deposits and its history with mining of the salt, and the towns of Middlewich, Northwich, Nantwich and Winsford are all key mining towns. "Wych" actually means "brine town". There is a lot of information regarding salt mining in Cheshire and the effects, some of the facts have been condensed down to give a good overview.

The salt was deposited during the Triassic period (200 million years ago) when Cheshire was an inland sea. This then evaporated leaving vast salt deposits behind.

At one time wild brine pumping was a popular way of extracting salt (particularly in the Northwich area). It involved pumping the brine and dissolving the salt along the way. Towards the end of the 19th century, wild brine pumping had disastrous consequences with holes appearing all over the area, creating flashes (large lakes) and swallowing up entire buildings. In Winsford, the notable "flashes" are Top Flash and Bottom Flash on the river Weaver, and there are also flashes at various locations around Northwich.

Winsford rock salt mine has a series of huge underground caverns running for miles, which are held up by pillars of salt to support the roof. The mine is next to the river Weaver, which was used at one point for transporting the salt. Mining began in this area in the 1830s due to the instability of the mines in Northwich.

The Romans were aware of the salt deposits, and there is evidence that they used lead salt pans at Middlewich, Nantwich and Northwich.

Cheshire Cat

Lewis Carroll (real name Charles Lutwidge Dodgson) was an English writer, mathematician, logician, Anglican deacon and photographer. He was born in Daresbury, Cheshire (near to Runcorn and also to Norton Priory). Cheshire was his inspiration for his most famous novel, Alice in Wonderland.

One of the most famous characters from his book is the Cheshire cat. It is best known for its big wide grin, and the way it appears and disappears. There are carvings of the Cheshire cat that can be found at churches in Pott Shrigley, Grappenhall and Macclesfield. There are also carvings in other parts of the country where Lewis Carroll moved to later in life.

However, the phrase "grinning like a Cheshire cat" appears to predate Lewis Carroll's book of 1865 and was a well-known phrase already. Some theories are that it originates because Cheshire cats were always happy to me among the milk and cheese from the extensive cattle farming in Cheshire. Other theories are that it is also because of the bowl shape of Cheshire, so it is like the milk (and the cats of Cheshire) are in a huge big dish.

Smuggling, Wrecking and Sea Folklore

In the early 19th century, Cheshire ranked just behind Cornwall as the worst place for wrecking and smuggling in England. The marshes around the Wirral were a good place to lure boats and ships in order to steal the cargo. Criminals would use lights in the fog to lure the boats the wrong way, and then would kill any survivors of the ship wrecked boats before stealing the cargo.

There was an inn called Mother's Redcap inn, where the incoming tide would bring boats right up to the door with illegal imports. It was a meeting place for smugglers and was also used as a storehouse.

Moving inland a bit, Northwich (one of the Cheshire salt towns) also attracted smugglers. Salt was a taxable commodity, so townsfolk wanted to smuggle it out of the town boundaries without paying tax on it. To do that, the locals would pack salt into coffins and drive the coffin on a horse and cart slowly through the town with a string of fake mourners following closely behind. The scheme worked well until officials at the town hall (where the funeral parades passed to get out of town) became alarmed at the number of local residents that appeared to be dying, and then figured out something wasn't quite right and checked one of the coffins.

Back to the coastline, there was superstition surrounding the people who drowned at sea. People believed that anyone who drowned at sea was a soul taken by the sea and if you tried to interfere with that, another soul would be taken instead; so some people were left to drown without anyone helping them. People would often throw bodies back into the sea because of that superstition. However, along some stretches of the coast, the folklore was that if you found a body you had to give it a Christian burial, otherwise the ghost of that drowned person would haunt you until the end of your days.

Hack Green Secret Nuclear Bunker

There is a "secret" nuclear bunker at Hack green, Nantwich, Cheshire. Amusingly, you can easily find it these days by following the numerous brown tourist signs for the "Secret nuclear bunker".

It remained secret for a number of years, and the vast underground complex (35,000 sq ft) was set to be the centre of regional government had nuclear war broken out.

Hack Green's involvement began in 1941, when the area was a decoy for World War II raids on the large railway station at Crewe (about 10 miles away). It then became a radar station. It was then turned into a blast proof nuclear bunker capable of housing 135 people for 12 weeks.

It has now been turned into a tourist attraction, and people can go down into the bunker itself.

Lady Beswick's Mummy

Gentleman (Highwayman) Higgins, had his body kept by a Dr Thomas White. This same doctor also had another body due to a rather unusual request.

He had amongst his exhibits, a mummy. This was not an Egyptian mummy, but an 18th century Cheshire mummy.

One of the doctor's patients had been a Lady Beswick. As well as a chronic hypochondriac, she was also very stubborn and awkward, and also had a fear of being buried alive. In her will, she named Dr White as her chief beneficiary and left him the huge sum of £25,000, on condition that he had her embalmed and kept her above the ground for a hundred years. Also once a year, Dr White and two others had to check that she was still dead.

The eccentric doctor had her embalmed "by the best techniques of Paris and London" and put her in the case of a grandfather clock and then stuck her out on his roof. When he died, the body was then moved to the Manchester Natural History Society and was dutifully checked on as ordered. Finally in 1968, the burial took place.

Lady Beswick had got her wish and stayed above ground for well over 100 years.

Bridget the Witch

Bridget Bostock was a white witch who lived in Coppenhall, Cheshire. She was hailed as a spiritual healer and was visited by people from far and wide.

Her healing powers came from her saliva that she used for healing, and she would lick the wounds to heal them (!). The National press heard about her mystical healing powers and she became very famous throughout the whole of England.

At the peak of her fame she was curing 160 people a week, and always refused to take payment for her cures. She had to hire a doorman to control the number of people coming to see her.

Nobody knows exactly when she died, but it was sometime in the middle of the 18th century. She had healed thousands in her lifetime.

The Statue Tried for Murder

In the tenth century, Cheshire was undergoing a long period of drought. Lady Trawst, wife of the Governor of Hawarden, prayed to the statue of the Blessed Virgin Mary for rain. Immediately a thunderstorm broke out and loosened the statue sending it crashing down on top of the lady.

The statue was tried for murder and sentenced to be hanged. However, this was an impossible task, so because burning it would be sacrilege, they tied it to a wooden cross and left it on the banks of the River Dee to drown. The current carried the statue and cross to Chester where it was found and taken to St John's. It remained there until the Reformation, when it was torn down and used as a whipping block.

The Prophet Robert Nixon

Cheshire once had its own Nostradamus in Over. He had a talent never seen before and could foretell the future.

Robert Nixon was described as a short squab fellow with a great head, goggly eyes and a tendency to dribble when he spoke. He was also very surly with a big gut.

Nixon was employed as a ploughman, but was terrible because he would suddenly stop work and stand in trances. One time, during the battle of Bosworth, he is said to have shouted "Now Harry, get over that ditch and you will gain the day". The only problem with that story is that he would not have been ploughing at the time of year that the battle of Bosworth took place.

However, Nixon did prophesise the fall of the last abbot of Vale Royal and the passing of lands. In time, the news of Robert Nixon's prophecies reached King Edward IV, who sent for him to come to London.

The king decided to test Nixon, he hid a diamond ring and asked Nixon where it was. Nixon apparently impressed the king by saying "He who hideth can find". The king then ordered that all Nixon's prophesies were written down. He also gave freedom of the palace to Nixon, who annoyed the staff because he sat there constantly eating and drinking.

One day the king was departing for a hunting trip and Nixon pleaded with him not to be left alone, otherwise he would never see him alive again and would be starved. The king then ordered an officer to look after Nixon in his absence. However, Nixon was mercilessly mocked by the kitchen staff who hated him, so the officer quickly locked Nixon in his room for his safety and set off for what he thought would be a quick trip with the king. Unfortunately the officer was kept out for three days, and when he returned Nixon was dead – starved to death. Another version of the story says that the kitchen staff were actually the ones who locked him in the room because they hated him so much.

During his short life, Nixon was said to have written down enough to for-tell the Civil war and the winning side, the death of Charles I and the Restoration of Charles II, the abdication of James II, the French Revolution, the Great fire and plague, and the accession of William of Orange.

There are existing memoirs of Robert Nixon, some in prose form and some in verse. Nixon remains a strange and fascinating character, with at least a grain of truth in his predictions: con artist or prophet – you decide!

Folly Mill

There are ruins in the valley of Clough Brook just before its confluence with the River Dane. The ruins are of an 18th century building called Folly Mill.

It was a paper mill that was built so deep into the valley that it was very difficult for horses and lorries to drag the raw materials down and finished products up again.

When it was first built, it was washed away. The owner Abraham Day then rebuilt it, but it was washed away again. When he started to rebuild it a third time, his wife threatened to go to bed and stay there if he carried on foolishly rebuilding it. He paid no attention and started to rebuild it again. His wife kept to her promise and retired to bed on that very day, where she finally died age 76.

The mill once again lies in ruins in the valley. The name folly was applied due to the crazy location of the mill that kept being washed away and that had almost impossible access.

Anderton Boat Lift

In Cheshire, there is an amazing structure that can lift whole boats (and the surrounding water) from one river up into a completely different river at a different level. The Anderton boat lift was built to lift cargo ships 50 feet from the River Weaver to the Trent and Mersey Canal. It was built by Edwin Clark in 1875.

The concept is simple; two large water tanks with sealable doors to carry the boats up and down. At one point the counter balance system was replaced by electric operation, but is now hydraulic again.

The lift operated until 1983 until the structure deteriorated. It was then restored in 2003. It is one of the popular attractions in Cheshire; you can take boat trips and actually ride up and down in the boat lift.

Mad Allen's Hole

Mad Allen's hole is a two-storey cave on Bickerton Hill (part of the sandstone trail –a Triassic sandstone ridge that runs across the Cheshire plain). The cave is believed to be the location of "Allenscomb's cave", in which an eccentric hermit, called John Harris, lived for 46 years. He was not discovered until 1809; four young men were gathering firewood for bonfire night, when they saw what they described as a wild hairy man; they fled to the nearby village of Harthill where they recounted their story about the wild man entering the rock face. The young men returned and found John sitting next to a fire; he told them he was 99 years old and told them his life story and how he came to live in the cave.

The hills around Bickerton also contain evidence of settlements going back to the Bronze Age. Nearby, there is an Iron Age hill fort called Maiden castle (dates back to 600 BC). This is the most southerly of the seven hill forts of Cheshire.

The History of the Stamford Lodge Site

The new Waters site in Wilmslow, Cheshire, is the world's largest single site committed to developing Mass Spectrometry systems. Mass spectrometry is used to safeguard our food and water supplies, protect the environment and advance healthcare.

Prior to Waters occupying the Altrincham road site in Wilmslow, it had lain empty for 10 years. The resident bats of the old Stamford Lodge were moved to an on-site custom-made bat house so that the new Waters facility could be constructed.

The site has a very colourful history and has had numerous occupants. It has been known by the name Stamford Lodge since at least 1842, where it appears on an OS map. The original building was thought to date back to the 1780s.

The lodge was once occupied by John Goodier, who ran a number of farms in the area. The land itself was owned by the Earl of Stamford (who lived in Dunham Massey Hall). The Earl of Stamford also owned land on the other side of the river Bollin and leased some to the Gregg family, who founded Quarry Bank mill on the land. Prior to that, there is evidence that other farmsteads occupied the Stamford Lodge site.

The lodge then passed hands a few times, with one owner being Francis Godlee, a Quaker businessman (of the Simpson and Godlee Cotton Company). Francis Godlee used Stamford Lodge for breeding horses, but he is best known for being a founding member of the Manchester Astronomical Society; he donated the Godlee Observatory, and telescopes within, to the city of Manchester in 1903.

The lodge was the first in the area to have electric light installation; even lighting the stables and outhouses. The building was extended and changed continuously throughout the 20th century. By 1939, Stamford Lodge was occupied by Sir Norris Agnew (chairman of the board of governors of the United Manchester Hospitals). The site was also owned by the Boddington brewery family for a time.

The area around the site has important historical significance, with the famous Lindow man being discovered in nearby Lindow Moss (the preserved body dating back to 2BC – 119 AD was discovered in the peat, and is now kept in the British museum. It is one of the oldest murder mysteries around!). All along the River Bollin, which flows near to the site, there were medieval mills. As an aside, did you know that the famous WWII code breaker, Alan Turing, lived and died in Wilmslow?

Peckforton Cyclone

Peckforton hill stands close to Beeston hill. Peckforton hill has a country house on top of it (built in 1850) in the style of a medieval castle.

On the evening of 27th October 1913, Stonehouse Lane was battered by the freak Peckforton Cyclone. According to an eyewitness, a dark column of spinning air approached from the south. It was accompanied by thunder, lightning and torrential rain. During four violent hours, Castlegate Farm, below Beeston Castle, lost its roof, hundreds of mature trees were uprooted, several cattle killed, and a local man hurled sixty metres into his neighbour's orchard.

An ancient oak tree, thought to be hundreds of years old, survived the cyclone with the loss of a few huge branches.

Cheshire Facts

- Chester racecourse is Britain's oldest sporting venue, with the first race occurring in 1539. The horse racing replaced a violent traditional local football event. The idea to change the sporting event was thought up by Mayor Henry Gee – hence the name "gee gees".
- Chester has the most complete circuit of walls around any town or city in England.
- A local tradition says if you can run the 108 steps in Macclesfield in one breath, then you can have your heart's desire.
- Chester's Rows are unique not only in Britain but (in this precise form) anywhere in the world. The covered walkways on four of the main streets of the city means you can shop on two levels.
- Bromborough in the Wirral is thought to be the first place the Vikings from Dublin ever settled on the English mainland. That ancient link is demonstrated with a Viking cross in the local church. A great battle in which five English kings died fighting the Norse and Scots was also probably fought here in 937AD, 35 years after the settlement was established. A buried longboat was recently discovered at Meols a few miles away.
- Cheshire's name is derived from an early name for Chester (Legeceasrerscir or *Cestrescir*) meaning the shire of the city of legions.

Old Cheshire Words

Cheshire word	Description
Agged	Tired
Arsemart	Knot grass
Baggs	Commercial traveller
Bandy Hewitt	An ill-favoured dog
Gollop	To swallow greedily
Skelp	To leap awkwardly, like a cow
Humpering	Walking lamely
Mort	Vast or a great deal (for example of money)
Poo	To pull
Strokings	The last drop of milk from a cow, said to be the richest part
Like (pronounced Loike)	An expletive, used in a sentence: I am like to do it)
Knocking up	A job back in the mills where someone would wake the workers up
Gob	A foolish person
Tupp cat	A tomcat
Wangle	To totter or vibrate
Lawyers	Long brambles in covers, from which you can't escape
Blart	To low like a cow
Cobnobble	To chastise
Cocket	Pert, saucy
Cowshat	Wood pigeon
Crumpsy	Bad tempered
Fac	Soil
Forkin robin	Earwig
Gammock	To fool around
Kazardly	Accident prone
Knobs	Lavender
Lancashire gloves	Hands without gloves
Licksome	Pleasant and agreeable

Muggin (to receive a)	To be beaten up
Mulsh	Drizzly weather
Rip	To speak vehemently
Smudge	A sponger
Cob	To throw
Swallowmass	A glutton
Whooked	Shocked
Titback	Horseback
Tooty pot	Hole in the road
Yobbins	Outcries, yells
All macks	All sorts
Bach	A fall or stream (as in Sandbach)
Bad luck top end	Someone who is crazy
Bang	To excel/beat
Bradow	To cover in manure
Chimbley	Chimney
Chump	A term of reproach, rascal, cheat
Chunnier	To crumble
Crap	A particular way to mend a clog
Dobbin	A timber cart
Hooter	Owl
Poop	To peep
Boggarty	Liable to take fright or too shy
Butty	Sandwich
Foxy	Wet, marshy
Powfagged	Exhausted
Cankum	A prank
Tom and Jerry	A public house
But	Unless
Graith	Riches
Meg Harry	Tom boy
Mulsh	Drizzly weather
Gafty	Doubtful
Glottened	Astonished
Harbouration	Collection

Riding the stang	Punishment where the offender had to ride a pole (stang)
Picking up	A term for picking a pocket
Skuds	Owl pellets
Stinking roger	Water figwort
cotquean	Man who interferes in women's work, especially in the kitchen
Fudge and fash	Nonsense
Riff raff or rabblement	The mob, the lowest orders of the lowest orders
whistle bally vengeance	Bad, poor quality beer
Mortacious	Very
nookshotten	Crooked, disappointed
cubberlin	Annoying person
Feck	An exclamation
Fasheous	Shameful
cobbst	Unruly (children)
Fleck	To catch fleas
Cocket	Pert, saucy, or in good health
Snitter	To creep or walk slowly
Crits	Small potatoes
Shakassing	Idle
Yell	Ale
Weaver	From the Welsh Wye Fawr "great river"
Shanks pony	To travel by foot
Rittling	The runt of the litter, smallest and weakest
Rotten	Rats
Gollop	To swallow greedily
Wench	Girl
Rute	To cry and roar like a spoilt child
Buck	Bread and butter
Hanna	Have not
Kerve	To turn sour
Dirty dick	The wild flower, goosefoot. Often grows on dungheaps.
Noup	To hit on the head
Feart	Afraid

Full bat	Quick pace, as fast as possible
Boosy cheese	Cheese made before the cows are turned out to grass (boose is a cow stall)
Bong	A river bank
Make	To go (as in "We're making to Knutsford")
Rough nutting	Going out to pick sweet chestnuts
Bloaten	To be very fond of someone
Flam	To deceive
Egg on	Urge on, encourage to do something
Fox	To pretend to be asleep
Overwhelt	A sheep on its back
Who	To make a horse stop (also spelt wo) or the whole of something
Powler	To thieve in a petty way

Bibliography

www.mondrem.net

www.wikipedia.com

http://www.archive.org/stream/glossaryofwordsu00leigrich#page/n5/mode/2up

http://mythsandlegendsofcheshire.blogspot.co.uk/

Woods, F., *Cheshire Ghosts and legends* (Countryside Books, 1990)

Conway, A., *Dark Tales of Old Cheshire* (Sigma Leisure, 1994)

Crosby, A., *A History of Cheshire*, Alan Crosby (Phillimore & CO. LTD, 1996)

History, gazetter, and directory of Cheshire (Francis White and co., 1860)

Bowerman, A., *Walks in Mysterious Cheshire and Wirral* (Northern Eye, 1990)

Curzon, J.B., *Hidden Cheshire* (Countryside books, 2000).

Gillet, J. (The Journey Man), *Cheshire Folk Tales* (The History Press, 2012)

Ref: Stamford Lodge, Wilmslow, Cheshire – A programme of archaeological works, December 2012, Alvaro Mora-Ottomano.

All photographs taken by P.Manley (author)

Printed in Great Britain
by Amazon.co.uk, Ltd.,
Marston Gate.